from

Austin

The Love Project

10/16/14

Also by Austin Straus:

The AI Poems
Drunk with Light (2002)
Intensifications (2010)

Also by Wanda Coleman:

Mad Dog Black Lady (1979)
Imagoes (1983)
Heavy Daughter Blues: Poems & Stories 1968–1986 (1987)
A War of Eyes and Other Stories (1988)
Dicksboro Hotel & Other Travels (1989)
African Sleeping Sickness: Stories & Poems (1990)
Hand Dance (1993)
American Sonnets (1994)
Native in a Strange Land: Trials and Tremors (1996)
Bathwater Wine (1998)
Mambo Hips and Make Believe: A Novel (1999)
Love-ins with Nietzsche: A Memoir (2000)
Mercurochrome (2001)
Ostinato Vamps (2003)
Wanda Coleman—Greatest Hits 1966–2003 (2004)
The Riot Inside Me: More Trials & Tremors (2005)
Poems Seismic in Scene, with Jean-Jacque Tachdjian (2006)
Jazz and Twelve O'Clock Tales (2008)
The World Falls Away (2011)

The Love Project
A Marriage Made in Poetry

Wanda Coleman
& Austin Straus

Red Hen Press | Pasadena, CA

The Love Project: A Marriage Made in Poetry
Copyright © 2014 by Wanda Coleman and Austin Straus
All Rights Reserved

No part of this book may be used or reproduced in any manner whatsoever without
prior written permission of both the publisher and the copyright owner.

Book design and layout by Natasha Castro

Cover art by Austin Straus
Authors' photos by Susan Carpendale and Rik Pagano; "At the Whisky A Go Go"
by George Evans; "Over breakfast in Eugene, Oregon, 2006" by Penelope Patrick
Oshatz; back cover color snapshot, family archive.

Library of Congress Cataloging-in-Publication Data

ISBN 978-1-59709-967-7 (tradepaper)
ISBN 978-1-59709-733-8 (clothbound)
The love project : a marriage made in poetry / Wanda Coleman & Austin Straus. —
First edition.
    pages cm
  1. Marriage—Poetry. 2. American poetry—21st century. I. Coleman, Wanda.
Poems. Selections. II. Straus, Austin, 1939– Poems. Selections.
  PS595.M3L68 2014
  808.81'93543—dc23
                           2013030244

The Los Angeles County Arts Commission, the National Endowment for the Arts,
the Pasadena Arts & Cultural Commission and the City of Pasadena Cultural Affairs
Division, the Los Angeles Department of Cultural Affairs, the Dwight Stuart Youth
Fund, and Sony Pictures Entertainment partially support Red Hen Press.

First Edition
Published by Red Hen Press
www.redhen.org

Acknowledgments

Cover Art: from *The Kiss*, a zinc-plate etching by Austin Straus, January 17th, 1985.

Epigram: from the poem "Be Near Me" from *The Rebel's Silhouette* by Faiz Ahmed Faiz, translated by Agha Shahid Ali 1991, Peregrine Smith Books, P.O. Box 667, Layton, Utah 84041.

Poems Previously Published by Austin Straus:

Grateful acknowledgment is made to the editors of the following magazines and anthologies where some of these poems previously appeared: *Asylum, CQ/California State Poetry Quarterly, The Minetta Review Literary Journal, Pinchpenny, Poetic Justice #13, Slipstream,* and *Stone Country.*

Poems Previously Published by Wanda Coleman:

Grateful acknowledgment is made to the editors of the following anthologies, books, magazines, and recordings where some of these poems previously appeared: *African Sleeping Sickness (Stories & Poems), The Archive Newsletter #45/Archive of New Poetry, Asylum, Berserk on Hollywood Boulevard, Cold-Drill, Dicksboro Hotel and Other Travels, Hand Dance, Heavy Daughter Blues: Poems & Stories 1968–1986, HIGH RISK: Anthology of Forbidden Writings, Imagoes, Jacaranda, L.A. Weekly, Los Angeles Times Magazine, Ostinato Vamps, Poetry Loves Poetry,* and *Stand Up Poetry.*

For our friends and lovers the world over

Table of Contents

I. The Husband
poems by Austin Straus

II. The Wife

poems by Wanda Coleman

III. About the Authors

Be here when night laments or sings,
or when it begins to dance,
its steel-blue anklets ringing. . . .

The Sacred Engaged—An Introduction

Marriage under the usual pressures of contemporary American life is difficult enough without crossing the divides of race, religion and culture; however, in our union we have done precisely that. It has been difficult beyond description. We have been acutely aware of the discomfort that most people tacitly or outrightly express when discovering that the Jewish man and African-American woman approaching the counter are man and wife. That discomfort (often disgust and ill-concealed outrage) has radiated strongly in the intimate circles of family and former friends. We have spent uncountable hours dissecting relationships in our analyses of who does or doesn't like whom for what reasons. We have intensely studied how our careers as writers and artists have been affected by the limitations of others. We have laughed or wept with amusement over such reductive labels as anti-Semitic, racist, womanizer and *schvartza*. Calling names is easy enough; separating the truths from the distortions is a complex and ceaseless preoccupation. Prior to this dual project, we have discussed the pros and cons in joining ourselves in places, to date, kept apart. The husband has had his creative turf, the wife has had hers. This, then, is our contentious yet loving dialogue through poetry—with one another, through one another. We are aware of the great risks inherent in revealing ourselves in ways that might be wiser to keep private. However, we have been public entities on the Southern California literary scene for three decades, and sacrificed many of our evenings for nearly fifteen years to share our love of poetry with our community over our Saturday radio broadcasts (1981–1996). Today we continue to share our poetry at readings, workshops, and on campuses. We have selected these poems to shape a dialogue that transcends us as individuals, to offer some of the better that has flowered between us as our gift to the world.

—Wanda Coleman and Austin Straus/Los Angeles

The Husband

poems by

Austin Straus

When You Know

what I know
and you have what I have
you don't advertise and
you don't brag; you just live it,
and even then, it radiates
and people guess and are jealous,
because you look too good,
too young, too *something*
they can't figure out; and
you know that you have it,
the mystery is no mystery
because you live it each minute,
and it's always there, and you try
to get it into your teaching, to
give others a taste of it, because
it's so good and important
you want to share it, but, of course,
it never comes out quite like
the original; and, besides, it's not
something you can just hand people,
words on a platter, like this poem,
merely a hint . . . and that's all I can do,
just suggest, and be who I am, with
my little box of secrets out there
for all to see, knowing what I know,
living it, being it, with you

Moments Like This

You make some ridiculously hilarious crack
while I'm driving, and I laugh so hard,
the tears blur my vision and I nearly
plow into a truck

or we're watching a flick and you notice
some anachronistic bit, like some building
that didn't exist in Los Angeles in
1956, and how do you know this?

or we get off the freeway in an unfamiliar
spot and I want to go right but you say
left and lo and behold, in a minute or two
we arrive at the place with no sweat

or you warn me about impending doom
on some job or to be careful around such and such
person or that some scheme I'm hatching
is not going to work and you're always on time

or you have a dream about someone you haven't
seen in years and the phone rings and
it's them or you say something about some odd
thing and voila, the next second, it's on the TV

or we've had a bad day, communication's broken
down, I'm feeling lousy and resentful, and there
you are, at my back, giving me a rub or a hug
and your love transfusion floods me, again . . .

Home

Is this place cursed? You swear
plants die here, mattress
soaked with long-gone lovers, ceilings
falling, stained and peeling,
gotta get outta here or crack, say
ghosts gobble up your dreams.

Is this place cursed? His portrait
on the wall, ring pinching
your finger, name on a kitchen cup,
scrawled across a clipboard,
deep in couch and bed and rugs.

Habits of panic, violence, rage.
Clawing for life among roaches and
mice. The same old rot, a house
that wobbles in wind.

I come to slay ghosts, make
flowers bloom, change
the pictures on the walls and
the ring that eats your finger.

I come to break chains,
smash bad habits, release
the pent-up sweets.

I come
to kill
the curse.

Pictures of You

"The thing is to paint as if no other painter ever existed." —Cezanne

1

You break no Kodaks, so camera
friendly, the lens loves you.

Painting is another story . . . you are
variegated, light and dark browns
tinged with ochres, reds, oranges, siennas,
umbers, maroons and salmons, all blended,
everything but green and blue! What you wear
changes your skin tone, and where you sit
and how you hold yourself, look up, down,
sideways, and your expression, sad, meditative,
thoughtful, worried, calm, delighted,
and is it sunny or shady or rainy, and
what's the atmosphere, the barometric pressure,
humidity . . . the very air and light change you,
my brown/black, Indian red, multi-colored,
multi-brained, multi-sensed multiple, my
million women in one, my elusive, changeable,
unpindownable, ever unpredictable, highly
unpaintable you.

2

No one ever saw an apple before
or that mountain

and I never saw you, try now
to see you as if no one
has ever seen you, see you new,
from every possible angle and
nuance, real and surreal, flat,
round and cubed, collaged and
montaged, in shadow and light, color
or black and white, etched, sketched
and painted, in delicate pencil,
charcoal and pastels, or hard, linear,
contoured, barely seen or superreal,
totally, to all your levels, with all
the depths, complexity, truth and care
you have always deserved . . .

Why Wanda Loves Austin

He knows how to live, spends a
day off digging old Bogie flicks,
skimming a book or taking
a stroll. Needs no dough
to be rich. The guy's got
class. Give him a day
not hassling a job and he
comes through like a trooper,
squeezes time's orange
each drop a jewel.

Watch him lounge back
in bed observing the Dodgers
clobber the Reds. He even lounges
like a prince. A world-class lounger.
Note the sexy way he lifts the glass
to sip juice, his
majestic élan with pretzels.

And last night at the club, did you
catch his finesse when he
stuffed pieces of napkin
into his sensitive ears? That's
some kind of genius!

He's so graceful
it's a pity Degas himself can't
follow him around sketching sculptures.

God! See him order dinner for two
at the Thai restaurant. His cool
authoritative manner. His
balletic chopstickery. The style is
awesome, the work of a master.

Oh he knows how to live, slurping up
baseball on color TV, munching cold breaded
trout, scribbling poems to his woman.
The man's a whiz and she knows it.
No wonder she loves him!

Poem on the Way to Work

Every routine fits, I adapt and
ride. Even love
becomes a well-known
robe. Dressed in your
smells, braving the sealed
bus. Los Angeles dangles
its flan-gold sun.

Passive within a shell of sky-worked
light, turning slowly
pearl. The routine
perfects, each nuance
a dig worth mining. Here
the craved adventure, here
the passion and the crunch.

To love you. To love you
well. To never stop
this sweet
routine.

Conscience

everything you've said is held against you
always

the ugliness circulates and recirculates
perpetually
like blood

everything done lives on inside, unchanged
unkillable

all the prickly flowers of cruelty
all the pungent blossoms of stupidity

over and over the clips replay, you
the reluctant star

try to sleep, and the images come at you
laugh and your head breaks

the only cure for this torture

love

Deep English

When loving and relaxed, we babble
in a tongue spoken nowhere and never
by anything human, the deep English
of the bone, the sounds our blood
makes when we're pressed together,
when we're in each other, a sensible
nonsensical improvisation, our own
unintelligible undercover love song . . .

In the Studio

There were days, years, lifetimes
when nothing he tried came together
but
once in a while for an hour or
a minute, he was happy, in his
element, surrounded by the tools
of his numerous trades

> pencils and pastels and paints
> papers and brushes and pens
> typewriter and notebooks and
> all sorts of inks and glues and
> crayons and boards and markers
> magazines and wallpaper books and

the sun
like his thoughts
struggling into life
through various layers
of smog

There were long passages of wordlessness,
puffing on his pipe, thinking of her,
planning poems or paintings or some combination
of both
or simply doing nothing, letting the familiar
room full of old work cloak him
with his best self's products, allowing
the trajectory of his days
gently to pull him toward wherever it led,
soaking in the look feel smell of his makings,
the good overpowering the stink, the whole
collage of himself being good

and worthy to work with no matter what,
that self (here its visible tokens assail him)

one he finally accepts and loves

even if only fleetingly, a shot of vodka
worming its way into the brain

so slowly, agonizingly,
how fragile and seemingly
ephemeral this terrible love!
how soon dissipated when
he answers the phone, leaves
the studio, when anything other
than love intrudes

flickers
as he lights his pipe again
flickers

stay with me forever
stay with me forever, now

never again to mistreat himself,
to forget who he can be—the walls here
tell him, the poems tell him—never again

and love is at the door
pounding, eager to help him remember
forever
who he is
who they can be
together

Choreography 101

1

we lug stuff with us
whenever we move
books and paintings and boxes
and boxes of junk, old poems,
manuscripts, magazines;
yet, these things define us,
our stuff all mixed
like blood or come,
our books and records
mingled like spit, like
a long, deep, tongue-involved
kiss . . .

2

You flash past, naked, brown, totally free
and I note your fluid motion, think
that one of the great unspoken lovelinesses
of marriage is this sweet, innocent nudity,
how we are two beasts in the wood,
so comfortable and natural around each other
that, at times, I just take for granted that
this big dark Rubenesque in-the-raw female
breasts and butt bouncing by me,
is my wife!

Love Is

a box of voices, a butt,
a nose, a touch, a song, a
torso's twist; love is
her sticking with me
though I hurt her, what
remains after burning
through the lies and
tentativeness and fear
of risk and that terrible
load of disappointment,
leaving only the pure,
hot glow of what it is
we've got . . .

Presents

I will give you some presents
none of which have been cut from my body.
Other bodies have been mutilated to serve you.
Anything you desire I will make every effort
to hand you, if I have it around.

Here is the nose of a saint. Here is the tooth
of a shark, the pistil of a rose, the dried
seed of a banyan tree.
Do not ask about symbols.
Examine. Enjoy. Hang them around your
neck, pelvis and calves. Juggle them.
Toy with them as you toy with all your toyables.

Here is eighteen dollars and thirty-seven cents
including tip.
Here is a clay sculpture of an erect penis.
Here is a box full of cowrie shells, peapods,
iron filings and maize. Here is an address book
of mine from 1959.
Do not try to understand.
Fondle. Tickle. Turn them around
as you turn around all your turnaroundables.

Here is a bottle of new wine, sweet, white and
fruity. Here is the cover of a lost book,
chipped, yellowed and barely legible.
Here is a photo of me age about six, skinny and
blond, flying a kite and laughing.
Here is a letter from a woman I hurt.
Ask no questions.
Treasure them as you treasure all your treasurables.

Here is a passage from one of my unpublished plays,
stamped on a metal plate, suitable for a paperweight.
Here is a scribble I did while talking on the phone
to a famous editor. Here is a lock of hair
from a dead rock star. Here is a shard from an
ancient mixing bowl, Cretan, date unknown.
No, please do not try to evaluate.
Simply hold these in your hands.
Handle them as you handle all your handleables.

Here is a polished bone of cow. Here is a
finely worked filigree of cut paper. Here
is a large letter B ripped from a billboard
on York Avenue and 86th Street, New York.
Here is a bag of broken, still useable, crayons.
Don't use them before you see them, together,
like this. Then move them as you move
all your movables.

May I wrap these in a blanket or
will you have a cart? Please don't laugh
or cry or scoff, simply take these offerings,
from me, now yours, given tenderly, with care.
Soon there shall be more, and more significant,
gifts. Love them as you love all your lovables.

Compatible

she talks her way and I talk mine but
speak the same
fuck

    our kisses and tongues
    meet and strike sweet
    tunes

        we dance
        in the same
        dialect

            and though we look different
            black and white, man
            and woman

                we speak the same
                fuck and smoke the same
                music

Minor Misunderstanding

I can't always touch you, not even with
a smile.

Words flutter like sick gulls or
dying butterflies.

You're in the next room, a thousand miles
away, or right beside me on another planet.

I'm too full of self-pity and hurt
to move my heavy tongue to say "I love you."

Rotten day at work, my boss a fool, traffic
infuriating, time an abused old whore.

Ah, to hell with it! We'll sleep and forgive.
Someday soon we'll kiss again. I guess.

Marriage

We bite big chunks out of each other's hides.
Teeth marks. Blood. Blood spurts
all over our lives. The hot dump
we call home fills with blood.
Blood on the walls/blood in the sky.
We kill each other over and over,
two warriors, two tribes, two nations,
two worlds permanently linked
by love and rage. I cling
to the belief that this can be
stopped, that it is unnecessary, that
we do not have to eternally tear each other
to pieces, glue ourselves back together,
tear each other to pieces again; I cling
to that hope, know we can be friends.
I do not leave, do not run or hide.
I stay. And it happens again. Yet,
I still believe, even as I bleed,
you bleed, we bleed, love.

Talk

Sometimes our talk is so open and free,
goes so deep, it's as if
I were speaking a diary,
and you answer intelligently,
with care and good questions and
comments and suggestions of your own,
with stories from your life that
relate to or illuminate or
parallel mine, and so this diary
has your voice, that beloved voice,
and laughs your laugh; you are
sitting there opposite me in the
living room, and the air is filled
with our chatter and laughter, our
always earnest and precious exploration
of each other's lives, another way
we find each other.

Contrapasso ~~Contrapasso~~ Contrapposto

Though there's a basic awkwardness
in all this, we balance
asymmetrically, a more
difficult, delicate and deeply
exciting sort of balance,
threatening at any moment to
collapse, keeping us nervously
alert but always extraordinarily
beautiful

Ruint

What's left squeezes out
a love poem to one who
flattened me.

I'm pussy-wrecked,
teeth marks/flesh burns/mouth
smeared with yours.

Spent and sprawling
across this bed
an unstuffed scarecrow
buried in breath.

You do me in, drain juices,
allow the world to fill me again.
I come back loaded.

Where are you? I miss you! Two,
three long hours have passed.
Your sweet stink fades from my beard.

Wake me again with crazy hit and run loving!
Grind me into the sheets, refuse to release me.

I love the way you ruin my day!

Alone

in our old house
I grope for ways to say
I love you.

When you're not here,
I try to work,
turn up the jazz,
drink lots of water.

Your things are
everywhere; the whole
place whispers
you.

I want to avoid
the usual cliches.
Your voice
in my mouth . . .

You're out, but
you're here, somehow,
a poem
filling this space

Not a ghost
or a face
but a palpable
presence

The way everything
is arranged; a hint
of your skin,
books and papers

You've held,
stuff you use
and love scattered
all over

My feeling for you
isn't made of words;
I breathe, see, touch,
and you're here . . .

Variations on a Theme of Shakespeare

My woman's thighs are big and brown
And when she opens them, I sigh
Lick my lips and dive deep down
To indescribable delights—I cannot lie

If hairs be strings of lyres
Then a sweet black symphony plays
On her beloved crown; she fans my fires
In sacred, secret ways

Her eyes are dark, as is her skin,
With a voice of jazz, untrained but dusky;
Short, juicy limbs, a butt made for sin
And a fleshy perfume, addictively musky

She's unique, amazing, half my life
My beautiful, sensual, adorable wife

Kill Me

with truths, tear me
to pieces with everything I am,
hold me up to myself so I'll
know, without doubt, what I've
done, who I've been, how I've
hurt you; flay me, flog me, make
me pay and pay again for stupidity,
sheer obtuseness, for
the curse of the macho ego,
for being deaf and blind;
puncture me with facts,
club me with possibilities I never
considered or dismissed without
thinking; show me over and over
where I went wrong, how
I led us to slaughter, how
I killed us and maimed us
until your relentless and
pitiless love resurrected me,
made me see myself and you, us,
made me yours.

Blind Date

I couldn't see you
because she blocked and distorted
my vision; I saw you through her
or her in you; I heard
her voice when you spoke,
read her mean motives
into your decent ones.
She was there with us
for too long; now,
though she still lives
somewhere, she's gone
from here and, at last,
I see you for your self,
and love you, now, as if
you were someone I'd never quite met . . .
loving you now, as I should have,
for the first and always time.

The Good Woman of Watts

She is so bone good
bad people use her, take advantage.

She allows plenty of slack
on the rope you will hang yourself with.

She has trouble imagining the struggle
we regenerates have, trying to be good.

She's no innocent, far from naïve.
Her truth keeps her going.

Even when she senses or knows
what you're up to, she's tolerant to a fault

Watches and learns, gives you multiple
chances to change for the better.

It's you who shoots yourself in the foot
or jogs off the cliff. It's you who screws up.

And it saddens her to see it. She
is so deeply decent, it hurts her

to see others fail, to feel
the causes of their failure; she strives

to illumine the roots of evil, not
even slightly tainted by its horrors.

My empress, my saintly beloved,
my woman, wife, Wanda . . .

On Reading Your Love Poems to Me

Proofing your latest collection
I find new poems that betoken
a more profound affection
than anything you've spoken . . .

Are you too shy or scared
to tell me straight how much you've cared
thinking, perhaps, that it'd swell my heads,
causing my portly ego to become too well-fed?

Please, my lovely, don't get me wrong;
I'd frame your lines up on my wall,
so moved am I by your dulcet songs,
better heard in print than not at all . . .

But oh how deeply I'd cherish, dear
some impassioned whisperings into my waiting ear.

Variations on a Theme of Shakespeare (2)

My lady's face is exactly right,
The eyes, the lips, the nose, the nares
Even the birthmark, her teeth so white,
Complete a portrait to which none compares

Her mouth's so soft, that when we French,
Whose lips are whose I dare not guess,
Our tongues connect in a delicious clinch
Deeply, sweetly, in a long caress

A magnificent, strong-boned face by Gauguin,
Medusa-haired, African wild, untamed, dark brown/red
My goddess, with a chassis shaped by Rodin,
Deep-souled, sorrow-hearted, intuitive genius-head

All this, a miracle in every line
and I still can't believe that she's all mine!

That You Love Me

me, of all people, I pinch myself,
it's a dream, how'd it happen, what
goober dust did I fling in your eyes,
what magic potion slip into your mind?

That you, YOU, love ME, the player,
the wisecracking, life-loving painter,
the dance-away fucker from Brooklyn,
the guy you thought was a fool and a nut

That crazy bearded long-haired poet
who hardly knew you, bruiting it about
how much he loved you, that weirdo,
that hotshot, yet somehow he got you

I got you, me, all the mes that are me,
we got you, the painter, the poet, the lover,
the jokester, the Jew, the Brooklyn-born
fast-talking extrovert, we all got you

And you still get confused about which one
I am, who you fell for, who keeps putting stuff
into your drinks to keep you enthralled,
keep you laughing and loving, keep you

permanently his

Certainties

As sure as anything/the sun
will rise/the seas roll
and break against old rocks
and grass grow and the moon

cast down its pockfaced grin
and men kill and love and die in pain
and howling babes birthed and sung to
and somewhere rain and snow and heaving

earth and cold winds blow and painters
paint and composers conjure music from
cacophony/yet I know this: as long
as I live and see and breathe and

reach to touch and hold, so long will I
love you

The Shape Of

my life, a shape too large to
contemplate, like millions killed
or the infinite universe.

I am having enough trouble
shaping a moment, the next
minute

as chaotic, as formless,
as vast, as unknown and
terrifying

as all the realms of space
or the labyrinths of
my woman's mind.

Recreated Man

To remake this self requires
more than superficial cutting;
bald and beardless? I'd still be
me, as I am me naked.
It doesn't matter what I wear;
I'm still me in tie and tails,
T-shirt and jeans, Bermuda shorts,
pajama bottoms, underwear . . .
all the dressing in the world
cannot disguise or change
the beating, beaten heart.
And that's the heart
of this hard riddle: unseen and
hidden changes, while the outer
slowly ages yet stays "the same,"
need more delicate surgery,
sharper knives and sharper thoughts;
I am, too slowly, maybe, changing,
becoming kinder, smarter, wiser,
even as I appear the same old me . . .
what irony! My pleasant front
always worked to mask nefarious
doings; now, it suggests a sweet
and saintly goodness. Same surface,
different person. And who knows this?
Only you and I, my Wanda.

Shot

A glance from you, my love,
can pierce me like a spear,
a poison-tipped spear from which
I could die ... and I have ... many times ...
and a word or two, a loud, harsh word,
especially, and I'm machine-gunned,
swiss-cheesed, a holey man
no longer able to talk or breathe,
though it happens so fast
my shocked blood freezes, forgets
to gush, I reel and collapse
in a hail of curses ...

You're a dead-eye, a keen markswoman,
a sureshot, and I, always,
an easy, bloated, asking for it, needy
target. You split the bull's eye,
flatten me with a volley of phrases,
right between the brain lobes, I'm done for,
done in, all done, done again ...

I give up. I will never again draw
against the quickest puns in the West ...
You're too fast, too sharp, too deadly,
know me too well.

The hell with the shootout.
Let's fuck instead.

Your Kiss

is somehow softer, now,
more intense; your mind/body
chemistry amazes me, how
your brain sends signals to
your lips, retexturing and
sweetening them, as your
love mellows and sweetens,
your lips, your mouth,
your kiss, a poem that says
you are, at least in this
instant, loving me MORE . . .

As If

I'm immortal, I squander
my days; now,
I stop. What do I
know? To love someone
unconditionally. To forgive
myself totally. To cram
as much life as possible
into each fleeting moment.
To make life art, full
of joyous significance.
To stay calmly alive,
with all parts working.
As if every second
mattered.

"With Deep and Abiding Love"

(a dedication from Wanda to Austin)

Abide: to put up with, tolerate . . . to wait
patiently for . . . to await . . . to withstand . . .
to remain in a place . . . to continue to be
sure or firm, endure . . .

All of these apply. You
put up with my inability
to love. You tolerated
my many faults. You awaited
my enlightenment, withstood
my onslaughts, my meannesses and
blindnesses. You stayed,
solid in your love, in your hope
and belief that I'd *see*. You
endured. And now, so will we.

This Moment

at the dining table, chewed and savored,
reverberating
in my skull, seeping into memory
staying forever

and when and if it ever dies, if
everything dies when the person dies, I
will feel the loss, somehow, a loss
to posterity, to the universe

of a moment that throbbed
with life, that was so exquisitely
itself, as Wanda laughs to a movie
in the bedroom, as sunbeams

stipple the backyard yellow-green,
and Dambula the cat sleeps beneath my feet,
and this warm cereal cooked for me,
with love by my love

goes slowly down, second by second,
year by year, filling me, becoming me,
turning me into someone old and new
at once, who was and is and will be

here

The Wife

poems by

Wanda Coleman

Creature of Two Worlds

not gravity. the weight of worry
holds me to earth

lately i am a dweller under music with antennae
and gills. i move with the obscene certainty
of instinct. with the rolling joyful glide of
sultry rhythms. a new form venturing
among coral

it is the swamp that feeds me. the bittersweet
things i find on the underside that scuttle
on the surface, wade helplessly in my path
grow without sun, thriving on the
Vulcanic radiance of meaning

not gravity. the weight of my desire
holds me to him

as we meet/the genetically programmed mating of
different species/a secret race which peoples
the Devonian doom of a subterranean past.
i am impregnated
with the memory of his longing

a weakened seed gains strength in my blood
takes root in my word as i crawl toward shore
and give birth

not gravity. the weight of ancestral
pain holds me to strive

to break free of a murky history to leap beyond
its fictions/brave the treacherous currents of

melancholy straits. propelled by blind
devotion i swim toward the unknowable

not gravity. love
weights me to earth

someone's brought in fresh cuttings

from a garden
roses daisies carnations/the startled eyes
of children tonguing for light

someone has opened the windows
allowed fresh air & sun into the room
put on classical music
and awakened a sleeping order

someone is in the bathroom shaving
just to look handsome for her

she scampers anxiously in a circle, confused
uncertain

she doesn't know how to act

what is it about us

is it your hair unruly defiant sable
against the comb is it

your half smile head cocked to the opposing shoulder
your hazel eyes lowered to a come-on

certainly that big red tongue
certainly that big red throb i love to ride into
wild wild tremblings surrounded/cloaked
in your numb lust

it is. yes indeed

your i'm-coming-to-get-you walk
your arms ape-haired and held 3/4s high
focused on the object demanding ambulation

recreating yourself with the castoffs of civilization
finding magic in the discards of kinkiness

in me. is it?

is it your heart unruly defiant
against my love is it

is it?

Dicksboro Hacienda, Hollywood USA

a postcard of wizardry & woe
no wait to check in

beneath the shadows of palms
she swelters. body heat = 105

they lay naked. sip cold beer over ice
too hot to mambo

guests crowd the faceless pool
and Latin disc throbs pierce the ears of *turistas*
at Berendo & Beverly

too hot to think

the queen of spades is numb
zapped by endless giving
the red king can't trumph enuff

spiny lime cacti in truck gardens
the metallic chatter as electric fans
bite the air. soured milk
from mama breasts
inspire baby cries—*siestas & dos equis*

too hot to dream

over 200 units of drama
each room a bestseller—each patron, poem

at this hotel
you sign our guest book
in blood & cum

Romantics

the world proves lovers stupid
who think love
transforms it

lovers then
fools then

                              he sees beauty in decay
                              rescues me from *la brea*

                              my eyes
                              the stars. too bright
                              my eyes
                              i can't see
                              lead me

                              against his shoulder
                              leaning
                              into him. he sweats
                              a history of pain

in the Filipino bar i drop 2 bits for 6 songs.
we sip cold gold beer
before shopping for food & the return
to feed the children.
we neck in public. the world
revolves round us

                              whirling

divinity = love returned in kind

2 bags of groceries & later, my meal
gives him heartburn at 4 AM.
gastronomic differences
congenital in origin

i must learn to cook for him

lovers then

he disdains my props. vanishes them: coffee, marijuana, librium
take me. i'm all you need. take me

> high. i leave this planet
> like vapor
> and marvel
> at stars
> so bright. the first time seen
> clear. intense
> i burn

fool then

Just Another Hollywood Summer

high noon on Mercury

soot and embers. 110 in the basin
i sizzle in my usual fat

the other crispy critters
commiserate. it's a real biscuit burner

he turns over to get even on his other side
there's a crackle, a sputter, a hiss
of steam. something flakes off
drowns in hot grease

oh, this is *nuthin'* he smiles
you should try New York in the 80s—it's much worse

Scylla & Charybdis

this Sargasso muddied with the blood
of a thousand variegated lovers
whirls and sucks

some whooowhee
a current obsessed draws him in
the promise of no escape (a tree long felled)

this woman deep water this woman siren
this man this war this man's voyage

so unlike Odysseus
she covers his head his eyes whited back
in crisis tongue slack, wordless
stiffened arms his body swirling
in the rigors his joining joy birth
drowning

flesh and the rendering of it flesh
and his surrendering to it. (sailor sailor
home. at last. for a pearl) laughter born of
release having encountered the monster, embraced
her been consumed by her come in her
wet sated whole and washed ashore

his names for my breasts

Dicksboro Romance

once an empty room

there are two locks but one key
multiple doors, one heart

two bite-size bars of soap

the new tenant pays rent in advance
moves in & takes over
fumigates for all the pests

redecorates
puts flowers in vases
his calm papers the walls
pale green vines undulate in blue latticework
over pink splashed with gold over cocoa thighs

fills her spaces with his presence
vacuums & cleans the rugs/her wounds

he has scrubbed her eyes till they sparkle
and draped her visions with rainbows

two aspen white guest towels

she's sound in his arms
rocking the sacred rock/holy embrace
his fay whine her fever sob
locked teeth to teeth

he cums. draws blood

at this hotel, discretion is our byword
we provide room service
& buckets of hot ice

Pigging Out

—for Austin

at the restaurant we sit down to wine
we are so hungry
the crisp appetizers/early loves
and lightly seasoned salad
we've developed appetites for the garlic & onion of life
gorging on a main course of dissatisfaction
over frustrated creativity sautéed in
economic plight
he chews over his Brooklyn childhood
i pick at the tedium of youthful Watts summers

we eat away the lousy jobs stunting our talent
we eat away the hot smog-filled day
we eat away the war in the headlines
we eat away the threat of nuclear holocaust
we eat away love-threatening pressures
we eat away the human pain we see/feel/
are stymied by

(pride is such thin dessert)

we eat until our smiles return
until fat and happy

He Takes Her to the Movies

at the walk-in concession counter his
arms surround and embrace. she jumps
unaccustomed to public displays of tenderness
it takes a moment to unwind
into his fold

he prefers chocolate to popcorn
she reminisces about drive-ins

revivals turn him on as do existential
European visions or comedies
with cultural references to the Catskills
or Brooklyn. she's keen on film noir of
the 40s and 50s—anything to escape
her umber skin for an hour or two

she remembers when they cost fifty cents
he remembers when they cost a nickel

sometimes one asks the other
"did i see that with you?"

in the theatre's dark she is
now and then startled by slight muffled
sniffles mid-scene. the glow from
the silver screen illuminates
his tears

after the movies
they hold hands

Moss Landing, November 1981

so cold so deep so gray so
i will never own a piece of this
northern California picture postcard

strange little birds flutter/anxious
hearts across wet sand

he poses. i snap the shutter
we want to fuck—there
against sea licked rocks

but we share this site with too many
and we are too poor to tourist

a kiss at least
sky sky i feel exiled to sky
unanchored, adrift
sky sky rain cloud sea
pregnant with thunder

so cold so gray so
Mu found

we drink the dove blue beauty
and pass

Of an Absence

his silence would've been manna. just to be together enuff.
he could sit and read a book or write or correct papers or
read the sports page, giving her stats on the playoffs. and now
and again looking up to see if she's holding up. or standing
beside her at the window looking out and below. it would be
nice to speak in soft concerned nothings rife with mutual
understanding. this difficult time for her made less difficult
by his sacrifice. to be near. she might hold his hand for
a second. or he might tell her there's something in the corner
of her eye. or smile to himself and remind her of time
precious time. he might kiss her to express his love and
irritate her skin with his beard. they could go down to the
cafeteria for her coffee and his tea. then return later to see
   how things have gone

Dicksboro Romance (2)

is anger
twists/distorts

we do the grand tour
in a season of pain

nerves worn red & raw
the stink of decaying tragedies

battered children greet us
clad in the rags of white civilization
great brown eyes beg coin
pink palms held upward in familiar prayer

we look beyond them to
million dollar deals, ice tea elegance
& freedom

upstairs our room is done in Kafka gray
& Uncle Sam red
there's much to be hung up & shelved
before the afternoon of swans

do not disturb

from the veranda the black queen
longs for an ocean dip, aware she can't swim
the red king serenades her
as love reverbs
she joins him for song & samba

at this hotel
we provide champagne, patina
& a plethora of memories

happiness costs extra

8 PM *Dispute*

featuring pain on drums
fear on bass
heartbreak on piano
jealousy on tenor sax

there isn't space enuff for us to blow
wah wah wah
and he say i don't play love enuff
he wants to know what to do
(whatever's cool)

a door slammed. a glass thrown
my eye blackens

i won't give

summer wind dance in the torn drape jazz

he won't give

winter light dance in the cracked glass blues
harmonic possibilities
discordant hope

what should i do? he asks, applying lots of hot
whatever's cool, i answer
and day comes to a bad jam
my jerks and clowns and muthafuckers
his bitch-i-could-kill-yous

whatever's cool

Afterwards We Make Up

blood among my tears

this is our room full of eyes opinions angers
we write out our texts here
i wear nylon he goes nude

volumes of ill-stacked books threaten to fall
brown terry cloth bath towels hug doorknobs
jazz aria or treatise/running lines define
our issues/marital strategy (status post-altercation)

the quilt a scripted passion. a ruthless shimmy
recovery uncertain. broken glass

our communication is punctuated by violence
the willful grammar of artistic insecurity
too many commas too many
exclamation points

ethnocentric juxta/my pink-brown labia quakes
under the assault of his obsessive Semitic tongue

as his philosophical disposition hardens
(synergism abandoned for more
solipsistic venues)

my body his again

San Francisco Travelogue 1982

10/13
8:30 PM
we hit 101 north high in the silly season
past miles of coastal land raped by arson

9:00 PM
on the radio theatre, alien flies
assume human form
plot to take over Earth

9:30 PM
in Camarillo we pick up a road buddy,
a lone rider in a crimson Volks
we trade lanes till Santa Barbara

10:30 PM
we hit sudden fog in Santa Maria
thick enough to tear. we follow the
red taillights of trucks/metallic slugs
oozing along the freeway

11:15 PM
into San Luis Obispo the fog clears
we pull into a ptomaine palace for grilled cheese
and French fries with catchup
he has hot cocoa and i do coffee

10/14
Midnight
fiddling with the dial i pick up the mighty 1090
broadcast from Baja, California
zappin' golden oldies from my pigtail days

he's taken the wheel and i watch the sky
taking in the constellations: the 7 Sisters,
Ursa Major/Minor. i knew them all once
as a kid anxious to swallow the universe
and there it is! the moon-shaped ball of
white-blue in the northern sky, shooting out a
tongue of white fire. and before he has a chance
to see it too, it disappears. my first UFO
a disintegrating soviet satellite? a galactic
mote dying in the stratosphere?

3:00 AM

the fog returns. we're tired. we pull into
Salinas and hurriedly find a dive where
truckers flop and shell out 32.10 for a scumbag with
tissue thin sheets. there's no heat. we spread
the sleeping bag out on top and toss restlessly
me keeping him awake with my terrible cough
and spitting up the flu

8:00 AM

he wants love but i'm too sick and it's late
anyhow and we better hit the road
due in at 12:30 PM to do the do at S.F. State U

11:00 AM

we take scenic route 280 in gasping
at the cold green-hilled landscape
wishing to be free to run these roads
to Brooklyn and back, travel, laugh
and fuck our way across the U.S.A.

12 noon to 2 PM
we clock in at the student union for the gig
and sit around waiting for it to kick off
the audience arrives and i'm center stage
it's a struggle against nasal drip & phlegm
hyperventilated and high with the experience
i go into a coughing jag and break for the jane

afterwards. i seek out his arms and we split
we haven't eaten yet and his favorite grease is Chinese

3:30 PM
we're lucky and find Hunan's empty.
we cop a squat and dine supreme: dumplings,
cold eggplant salad, harvest spareribs, scallops
in crab sauce, rice. for dessert we buy the cookbook
and uhmmmm—the bouquet of flavors/blossoms
anew in our mouths hours after

6:30 PM
we've oohed our way through Chinatown
in and out of shops filled with high-priced
objects of cherrywood, ivory, china, lapis and jade
we make our way toward North Beach where i can't
find an old coffee house haunt so we settle
for an expensive little Italian cafe for
cappuccino and cheesecake New York style

we amble back to the car, daydreaming. it's
getting dark and we're wired/tired only 4 hours
sleep. i'm sicker and he's had it. we could impose
on friends 'n' such, but it's better to be alone this time

when we get to the garage i panic. i've lost my keys
30-odd keys and a blue whistle on 3 rings! i *must*
be sick. we rush out and retrace our steps

8:00 PM

it's cold and dark and we still haven't found the
keys. driving in this city is insane. you can't go
around a block. we move on the chessboard
knights in combat up 2 over 2 and back 2
it's colder. i stand in a doorway while he
jousts a phone. the Turk Street Y has a bath
& shower for two but he don't like the territorial scuzz
up aways we find the Embassy Hotel, park & get room
505 for 35 crackers with color TV and a bucket for ice

10/15

1:00 AM

can't sleep. sick and coughin' like it's gonna
croak me. he can't sleep. he's up worrying
i hyperventilate again/trouble breathing. rib-cage
muscle ache. the emergency room is 3 blocks away
we run there, it's faster to run. the lady M.D. tells
me it's flu residue. she has an Rx that'll fix
me quick and i laugh because it's my allergy Rx
i've had all the time but didn't know it could help

while i'm in check he's gone to get the car
he helps me in. and on our way back we get lost
trying to find the Embassy. he turns up one one-way
street and down another. i say go this way and he
goes that way. "fuck!" he says and turns the wrong
way down a one-way street. there's no traffic except
one car coming head-on. a cop. he puts

the red light on and pulls us over. "my wife she's sick.
we're out-of-towners." he warns us and lets us go

2:00 AM
back in 505 we prepare to bed. i sip water and
take a pill, apply camphor rub and his concern
my cough quiets and we sack out. finally

8:30 AM
i awake. he sleeps on. i lay for two hours
thinking it over. will it last this time?
when we marry will it keep? how will
the years wear us?

Noon
post glorious fuck. we clean the room & pack
downstairs in the bar restaurant
we discuss male-female violence, rape and the
death penalty over hot bread and omelettes

he loves this city. it's like his native New York
we must come back here. maybe to stay

we search for the keys one more time

1:00 PM
he rescues my keys in the garage where we
parked on Vallejo and Green. we hit the 101
southbound and laughing at our luck

2:30 PM
in Santa Clara we stop for trail mix, apple juice
and pumpkins for the kids and a copy of the

San Francisco Examiner with an item about the soviet
satellite's fiery return from outerspace
and the discovery of Marilyn Monroe's diary

3:30 PM

we hit King City the West Coast ticket trap
sure as i've predicted the highway patrol swoops
in for the pinch. it's been reported that
we're swilling wine in open defiance of the law
the chip gets embarrassed when we show him the jug
of apple juice. 2 prime suspects go poof!
so he cites us for speeding

8:30 PM

he's been sweating the wheel since 6 miles north
of San Luis Obispo. it's pitch dark and the oncoming
lights are too bright. the heat's risen 30 degrees
we're cooking by the Ventura county line
our wonder has long since become work
his eyes strain as he takes the miles. i count them
one by one. can't wait for home. on the radio we
catch old tracks of Make-Believe Ballroom

9:15 PM

we are suddenly assaulted by the overwhelming
stench of cow shit. we've hit Los Angeles County
the madlands of Hollywood on the horizon
home and no, the kids haven't missed us. hungry
we beeline to Vim's for a Thai dine to cap off the
trip. he spends his last bucks for the fantastic feed

road rats. plenty crazy plenty love

San Diego

"the light is like this
in the south of France," he says

we stand on the pier
watch the blond boys afloat
with their surfboards
waiting to ride the big wave

"here i can be somebody," he says
a wave comes and two of the boys take it in
the boys. how well tanned they are
with skins the color of wet sand
poised unconcerned
in Aryan uniformity

"you breathe better here. the air
is pure. we can rent a house off the beach"

we listen to the roar
another wave. more boys take it in
my heart hangs ten, braces with the wet thrill
of foam as they splash graceful
into the shallows

"you can find work here easily. me too," he says
i answer absently, my eyes on the blond boys
"this is a military town, full of rednecks
a tougher lily-white town than the one i come from
and i don't swim"
satin slate pelicans perch atop the lamps
that dot the pier. charcoal and enamel gulls dive
back and forth ocean-side

and cream white crests of waves crash
along the most unspoiled beach i've ever seen

his eyes my eyes. his lips mine
afterwards the light is brighter. we look out
into the rainbow of blues greens and aquamarines
watch as laughing swimmers return

"i guess you have a point," he says
we make our way silently along
glistening rocks. the waves roar

i pick sand stones
to carry home

Meanwhile in Manhattan

bad sushi

the future takes a bullet. on the A-train up from
Atlantic City we escape coal-stained urban granges/the
backwashes of failed industries and polluted truths. we
head north on the overground railroad seeking

the mythical pouch of his gestation/stone mother gargoyle
whose million-nippled breasts eternally nurse
the skyline arms extended in the gritty girth of her
tortured promise. we enter at Penn Station greeted by
shit-stained stumblers in shadow spurring on the
unreachables with croaks of "spare change"

my name password for excitement

we have come here a la crusade to find and confront—
mission irascible make some kind of connexion
between then and now when and how (seek and deplore)
his long mink hair streaming behind him i trail him in my
sleepwalk our soon-to-be-aborted child a pernicious hunger
denying me sleep—our stillborn success

steel papered in major and minor agonies the cacophony
of light bulbs shattering in street lamps *zzzttt* of the
red hotel neon sign peeping thru torn oilcloth window
    shades
the blessed hum of elevators zinging upward to
righteous oblivion or plunging downward to "where the
par-tay's goin' on" or

my name is woman-has-no-mind-left

next the ritual of exchanging banalities over expensive
cheesecake that's thick cool porous and flavorless
knowing secretly it's run by a corrupt union
even sweetness is on the take. but Empire State is still
full-flower the Flatiron Building as wedged and flat
Central Park is central to the point as ever even if
Ms. Statue of Liberty has taken hiatus for a skin bleach

(i wonder when i'm gonna see that massive sea of white
flesh congesting cement from 42nd to Wall Street—all
those gentlemen blondes prefer. all i see are niggahtoes
or variations on dark ethnics down-home uptown Blacks
from Africa, Indonesia, the Bahamas, West Indies, Fiji—
Buddhaheads and Spics—it's all *us* as if the Conk has
either become extinct or taboo)

holy mackerel my name chanted from Brooklyn's bridge

we hole-up in a high-rise war zone where the shell-shocked
and renegade reconnoiter marking time with speculations on
spurious victory. we bribe the guard with forged
        prescriptions
hiding our insolvency rather well. if only we had a criminal
conspiracy to tighten our game if only we lived as boldly
as we hope if only we had that killer distingué

my name is bitch-don't-you-understand

in latter-day rain all cabs are occupied by petite well-heeled
gray ladies busily plotting the overthrow of night-blooming
muggers. we hail and are stymied we hail and are stymied
we hail and he madly dashes for The Last Taxi on Earth

but Joe Senior stops him jousting and jostling for the ride
as i climb over them into it and send old Joe sprawling
with my booted feet

unkosher wine in bag we visit the studio of the Sculptor-of-
Breasts for a crash course on Jewish Holidays. then we
drop in on a cadre of word banditos crammed into a
junked-up den on the kinky outskirts of literacy/crib of his
third birth. challenged to defend the steatopygia typifying
women of my race i explain it eliminates the need for
pillows during sexual intercourse

my name is Sorceress of Muntu

we spook squid tanks in Chinatown, Fifth Avenue
patisseries, the crawls of SoHo, Hudson Riverside haunts.
we dig the fabled Chelsea and the profane Dakota. (we
Ham it up in Harlem in front of the Apollo/photo/me on
his lap/we're immortalized in wicker. we eyeball the
East Village, Christopher Street crannies, then Little
Italy where hostile ebony winos armed with squeegees
demand quarters

he spits my name/a wad of ill-chewed stuff

during his flip-flop there's nuthin' for me to do except
eat and see the sights. history takes hold. George
Washington squatted on the high-priced hole where i
discover All-American sesame flatbread. later i will be
found glass-deep in the 20-inch video watching greed
images set in miasma while uptown he frantically strip-
searches new-age social workers for contraband fatherhood

emotions held hostage our visit to Egypt at the
Metropolitan is a jizzmic rush/twenty-six galleries of
archaeological theft/my ancient blood-ties i fight the urge
to genuflect fight my tongue it seizes his/we ignite necking
among gold artifacts scarabs and urns our only wealth
a rich mutual insatiable lust

my name a whisper at twenty after midnight

underneath it all urbane garbage rages the rot of
     unresolved
dilemmas hearts rubbed raw toothy flea-ridden fears nesting
behind skin-thin walls the sewage of naked neuroses
rising wind-chill factor dealing in hallucinogens
smirking visions dancing on the third rail. bad sushi

my name is more than he'll ever know

Jazz Wazz

my heart in my ear his baby we need to talk jazz
later as in after the rain sleeping in the ghost
of his arms the essence of a beard tickling the roots
of wag about jobs not gotten and the life i'd live if
only you'd get with it jazz couldn't fill enough hours
trying to avoid the phone that did not ring the letter that
didn't arrive the love that was not stolen in sufficient
quantities. oh i said and oh the mirror answers
each time we pretend you are never on my mind

Ayin or No One

wind or voice of god?

the well-traveled road out of eden turns upon itself oases layers of elaborate multicolored sheets the way flesh dampens and gives burst to salt in excessive heats dilated eyes roll up and inward to whiten to circumscribe their own final shutterings windows boarded up nailed against intrusive harsh abusive sun against dust from unpaved roads snaking unwinding across three thousand miles of concrete majesty and fifty-odd years of thrashings up the amazon of the soul to her narrow darkened pathway jungled-down and threatening where she waits breathing deeply air of hunger vamp-shaman jihad-monger mother-of-the-city maker-of-roads her emotive tar sticky in the siroccan blaze captures the imprint of his eagerness his steps this traveler (fleeing holocaust) he's come in exploration/hadj the metropolis this ageless romance a shanker a miracle cause for shame cause for glory such fevers such contraindications/neuroses

"is the glass half full or half empty?" he asked.
"it depends on how thirsty i am," she answered.

the road ever onward the traveler naked and blind (nakedly blind) in lust an elongation that stiffens with satori drums drumming intensifies the act an unwinding turning in into her pomegranate eyes her raven mouth the cave of the giver crypt of the taker her holy hole thru which he simooms pain enduring forced labor the by-product of their night's cabal the childstuff suctioned from her womb into a necrotic blackness ever stillborn harmony the abortion/disembowelment of song frustrated/choked by the twisted umbilicus of hate his hardness the stubborn thrusts which storm her eyes flood her backwater dirt roads to spiritual el dorados the greedy claw of anger mauling her slave's heart as abusive as that urban sun endless poverty her eyes closed in wonder/submission to his davening the savour of his red sweat stinging her bluesy lips his hazel eyes relentless harmattans (he mounts he enters he descends) as on sheets twisted back on butt-weary mattresses stinking of generations of excessive demands tongue and again tongue their frictions one traveling flesh of the other over and over this ritual coitus/rendering of

delirium

Essay On a Marriage

she thought she was breaking in. he informed her
that she was breaking out, or
as one philosophical soul posed the issue

is the core half water or half antifreeze?
how does one who is heartfelt know emotion exists?
which came first—desire or the object desired?
if no one hears the crack is the heart broken?

acrylic and oil on canvas. a hardness inside a softness

then there was
that silver-haired couple—St. Louie lovebirds
who fluttered at the soirée like beached pelicans.
"he used to be a big shot in the math department,"
someone whispered. "they were always at events
like these," said another, "and kept up the habit."
the young gossips watched as he gesticulated to a
neophyte in a dark corner, while cronelike she helped
herself generously to the buffet, fixed plates for later.
"now," another chimed, "they sleep in their car.
he saved nothing for retirement. she never worked.
his social security is all they have."

is this a sinkhole or an exit bay?

she rarely sleeps naked but the climate
is warmer now, his night made difficult by
separation anxiety dreams. she too dreamed—
but of bookcases and strange men in trench coats.
they make love first—she cums, he follows—
and discuss sex afterwards, bodies still luminous,
thoughts congealed. Sunday morning wanes

quickly as they recover. they eat late, talk
and laugh into the afternoon. he grades papers
till dawn. she obsesses over well-known absences.

hands joined. they have red in common

there. in the basin
two throbbing organisms

Lay

enuff gloom & trouble
pained speculations hesitations expectations
aggressions & aggravations

enuff period

we have two lives on the cat
we've ridden experience wild woolly & ragged

been thru it

damned & damning

enuff
let us fall
      into red oceans of the other
get lost in our hungry skies/dreams/visions
         entwine/buried
      in blood black earth our flesh
let us burn
      stir our ardent ashes
      come impossible to separate

what i know of my man

how his head turns when desire enters his mind,
how he smells me how my smell arouses, how he absorbs
my breasts legs buttocks, how my feet, hands and nails
evoke touching, how the color and textures of my skin
agitate, how in black lace i stir his saint, white
his beast, red the john, blue the romantic,
how his eyes experience and transmit entry imagined,
how his ears taste my hot breath and listen acutely
for expressed fantasies, how his nose opens, how
his too moist mouth broods over my nipples, how his
dickhead tears in worship, how he sometimes pauses
to savor my anticipation, how his adventuresome
tongue explores and excites my rapture, how his
blood rushes, how our bodies glow together,
how friction exacerbates his final exquisite suffusion

baby baby

A Romantic Marriage

the bat in the skull. soul & sweet amber wine
ball-and-chain diary
every nook contains formulae for lust prolonged
step by step. vacant examinations

down to the nakedness, beneath the skin
like his cock, his hard rhymes have found me
and work through me to the p-bone

he exits the premises, the door open
leaves blown in off the walk
shadows thrown in the dim light of overcast suns
these bewildered agates locked on the past
the heart interred

discover this body is haunted

Give Me Time

—for Austin

give me jazz afternoon
give me slow sun in a glass eye
& a long drag on a j of bo
give me deep breath deep breath deep breath
a sip of California May wine
give me a reflective mocking smile
& breath. a deep breath
another catch of sweet sun
another toke on the j
more wine California May wine
turn up the jazz
another breath. dancing
a breath dancing in the wine
high. tension gone
the sun smiling in the jazz
this afternoon
thinking of you. and laughing
as breath comes sweet as wine
California May wine
and thoughts of loving you
take me so high
even jazz can't go there

White Wall Syndrome—A Study

a)
i sit here like a wound and weep
(a raw treatise on the release of shestuff?)
our accounts are maxed and there is no
assurance that we'll best the odds. nothing
guaranteed as we dance the rim of the brink.
i pay dues to craft organizations that
cannot guarantee me work
or recognition. i belong to the legions of
the heartsick who have no place to
take their grief, core organs dammed,
resenting ambiguous talk of a future

b)
i wonder when so-called friends
don't respond to letters, or return
calls. perhaps they have tired of my
chronic ravings, regard me as a persistent
dreamer and believer in an essential
but unobtainable good—perhaps view me
as an avant-garde hoodoo woman, casting spells
that entangle cumfreaks & Ur-chasers

c)
periodically, i recall the kisses of a man lost to me
whose lips were as thick and intoxicating
as the glue he sniffed. i see him now, hippling
the avenue, across the tracks, an elongated S
curved into the night, huge hand grasping that
stubby brown bag wrinkled at the crown,
as he dangled, nose down, tickled in the poison
that scrambled his words and, likewise, my heart

d)
when i am by myself, i notice that something
inside is dead. i am attempting resurrection

e)
the sheetrock has eyes that follow me
everywhere i go, to the kitchen, to the bathroom
where i take long soaks and
scrub my brownness raw with green soap
and mint leaves in late winter afternoons. they

peer from the bedroom's whiteness
watch me moan under his attentions
which i've done for many years—now,
spying as he spills his happiness into
my willful devotion. and later—as we snore—
pry into our love-spent swoons

f)
i don't want to fuck anyone but him—now

g)
he is of Jupiter. he thrives on enormity. he crushes
the small hopeful things that come within his orbit.
the satellites trapped and circling are coldly inhospitable.
but i know rivers of hot sulfur course beneath his
rainbow-hued crust of storms. that life, while bearing no
resemblance to how i have preferred it, exists
within this thorny creature of traumas and scars

h)
his face, beard and all, charges my softness with devilish radiance

Darwinian Ebb

what was there to begin with
nature in the foreground/unseen things sensed
resistance, therefore, without doubt
a scene where demonstrable horror is linked
to a minimum of means, the glimpse of a shadow
something seen but unrecognizable
in its imposing intimacy

out beyond Orion or encased at the onionlike core
of the self examining itself
one existing without the other yet in perfect if immaterial
correlation/lyricism unleashed and fragmentary
spotting the skin psyche/a form dissolving as it travels
room to room, breast to breast
vision recreating vision—the shapelessness of change
metamorphosis comes
reaching toward the whole imagined
a broken entirety

how much of the future is missing?
whose past is found in that simple black stone on the sand?
seeing with the heart keeps
form out of character, preserves
the image in the light—divides
this moment from that ancient wholeness

in which we were captured in the margins
and breathed one breath

Sonnet for Austin

—after a line by E. Ethelbert Miller

I love you as the grave loves the stone

I do not love you as if you were salt-pork or opal
or the sorrow of grass widows tending fields.
I love you as uncertain fingers foil tenderness
in public, where all eyes witness our covetings.

I love you as the wind loves the tumbleweed
and carries it across the sand to its lair of secrets.
I love you as chocolate loves cinnamon risen
from my breath to revive the poem in your eyes.

I love you as today loves yesterday—the way Billie loved Prez

With profound regret, I have to report that my beloved wife Wanda Coleman died on November 22, 2013 after a long illness. She had been eagerly looking forward to doing readings from this book with me but all her hopes for the future were, unfortunately, permanently interrupted.

She will be missed by all whoever knew her and/or her work and dynamic performances.

Wanda dearest, you will always be with me

Love, Austin Straus

About the Authors

Beyond Romeo & Juliet: How they Met

Poetry and art drew them together. In the spring of 1981, Austin Straus was the director of a poetry reading series at the Felipe de Neve branch of the Los Angeles Public Library. He had become active in L.A.'s new literary and spoken-word boom and was making his reputation as poet and visual artist. Wanda Coleman, a poet and writer, worked full-time in a medical office as secretary-receptionist. She had long distinguished herself as one of a new generation of poets fostered by the Beyond Baroque Literary Center.

Austin and Wanda had been married twice to others and divorced twice. The two had interacted briefly at various poetry circles, but were dating independently; she had read in his library series, and they had even danced together at the 30th birthday party of poet Laurel Ann Bogen. At yet another party, Wanda had discovered Austin's artistic gift, admiring his unique sun etchings. However, it would take yet another series of poetry readings and one more party to unite them as lovers.

Early that year, poet Elliot Fried's anthology, *Amorotica: New Erotic Poetry*, had been published. Elliot had set up readings by contributors— including Austin and Wanda—at three local venues. The last of these events was followed by a May Day celebration at Elliot's home in the nearby city of Long Beach. They would leave that party together.

———◦———

And when Love speaks, the voice of all the gods
Makes heaven drowsy with the harmony.
        —Shakespeare, *Love's Labour Lost*, IV, iii, 342

Our Movies

A Streetcar Named Desire
All About Eve
Babette's Feast
Being There
Black Narcissus
Casablanca
Death in Venice
Deliverance
Double Indemnity
Elmer Gantry
High Noon
It's a Wonderful Life
Key Largo
Kwaidan
La Strada
Laura
Let's Get Lost: starring Chet Baker
Les Enfants du Paradis (Children of Paradise)
Mildred Pierce (1945)
Pixote
Radio Days
Some Like It Hot
Sunset Boulevard
The Day the Earth Stood Still (1951)
The Third Man
The Triplets of Belleville
The Treasure of Sierra Madre
Twelve Angry Men (1957)
Vertigo
Wings of Desire
Witness for the Prosecution
Who's Afraid of Virginia Woolf?

Our Songs

Black Coffee (Peggy Lee)
Canto a La Vueltabajera (Alfredo Valdes)
Chelsea Bridge (Ben Webster, 1964)
Cherry Pink and Apple Blossom White (Pérez Prado)
Corcovado (Getz & Gilberto)
Crazy (& anything by Patsy Cline)
Daydream (Duke Ellington)
Ev'ry Time We Say Goodbye (Julie London, Charlie Haden)
Flamenco Sketches (Miles Davis)
Gnossienne No. 3 (& anything composed by Eric Satie)
Harlem Nocturne (The Viscounts)
Here's to Life (Shirley Horn)
Holding Back the Years (Simply Red)
I Didn't Know What Time It Was (Ray Charles)
I Like the Sunrise (Kurt Elling)
It Was a Very Good Year (Frank Sinatra)
Just the Two of Us (Bill Withers, Grover Washington Jr.)
Leyenda (Segovia)
Love and Happiness (Al Green)
Lover Man (& anything sung by Billie Holiday)
Lush Life (Coltrane & Hartman)
Nature Boy (Nat King Cole, Kurt Elling)
Ring of Fire (Johnny Cash)
Sexual Healing (Marvin Gaye)
Skylark (K.D. Lang)
Sweet in the Mornin' (Bobby McFerrin)
Take Five (Dave Brubeck)
These Arms of Mine (Otis Redding)
Valparaiso (Sting)
Wicked Game (Chris Isaak)
Winelight (Grover Washington Jr.)
You Go to My Head (Sarah Vaughan)

Photograph of Wanda Coleman circa 1991 by Susan Carpendale.

Wanda Coleman

Wanda Coleman was born in Watts, California in November, 1946 and raised in South Los Angeles. Her honors include the 2012 Shelley Memorial Award from the Poetry Society of America, fellowships from the California Arts Council, the National Endowment for the Arts, the Guggenheim Foundation, a Djerassi Institute residency, and the 1999 Lenore Marshall Poetry Prize, presented by The Academy of American Poets for *Bathwater Wine* (Black Sparrow Press, 1998). Her *Mercurochrome: New Poems* (Black Sparrow Press, 2001) was a bronze-medal finalist for the National Book Award. She was known for her live performances and has shared the podium with cultural icons such as Timothy Leary, Alice Coltrane, Allen Ginsberg, Bonnie Raitt, and Los Lobos. She appeared on numerous spoken word CDs including *High Priestess of Word* (New Alliance Records) and *Twin Sisters* (with Exene Cervenka, Idiot Savant Records). She was a former columnist for *Los Angeles Times Magazine* and had been an occasional contributor to The Poetry Foundation's *Harriet* blog, and an occasional one to the blog of David R. Godine, Inc. She was featured or profiled in *Writing Los Angeles* (Library of America, 2002), *Poet's Market* (2003), *Quercus Review* (2006), and *The Los Angeles Review* #6. Her short stories appear in numerous anthologies and literary magazines, including *African-American Review*, *Obsidian*, and *Zyzzyva*. She won an Emmy as a writer for *Days of our Lives*, and was twice a finalist for Poet Laureate of California. She was the first literary fellow of the City of Los Angeles Department of Cultural Affairs, and a Gaea fellow at the Sea Change Cottage, in Provincetown, MA. Her recent books of poetry are *Ostinato Vamps* (2003) and *The World Falls Away* (2011), both from University of Pittsburgh Press. She was a member of Budd Schulberg's Watts Writer's Workshop and an original member of Beyond Baroque's legendary Wednesday Night poetry workshop (1968–1971). She received the 2013 Book Award from the San Francisco State University Poetry Center for *The World Falls Away*. Wanda Coleman passed away on November 22, 2013.

Photograph of Austin Straus circa 1993 by Rik Pagano.

Austin Straus

Austin Straus was born in June 1939, in Brooklyn, New York. He has lived in Southern California since 1978. His poems and illustrations have appeared in numerous literary magazines and anthologies, including *Alcatraz 3, Black Bear, Caliban, Confrontation, Cottonwood, Grand Passion, Jeopardy, The Maverick Poets, Men of Our Time, New Letters, Plainsong, Stand Up Poetry*, and *This Sporting Life*, among many others. He is an accomplished painter, printmaker, and book artist with work in several private collections, including The Ruth & Marvin Sackner Archive of Concrete and Visual Poetry. His one-of-a-kind books combine poetry and graphics, and are in collections of The Athenaeum Arts Library, Chapman College, The New School, Occidental College, Otis College of Art & Design, the San Francisco Museum of Modern Art, Stanford University's Special Collections, Mills College, and others. His honors include the One Man Show: "Austin Straus—Collages: Word + Image," an exhibition and poetry reading at the Beyond Baroque Gallery in Venice, California; and a 1997–98 "Writers on Site" Residency, sponsored by Los Angeles County Museum of Art (LACMA) and Beyond Baroque Literary Arts Center. He frequently, informally, exhibits prints, drawings, and paintings in conjunction with readings. As the host of Pacifica Radio's *The Poetry Connexion*, he directed the show on KPFK from October 1981 through June of 1996 with co-host Wanda Coleman. *Drunk with Light*, a book of poems, was published by Red Hen Press in 2002. *Intensifications*, his second book from Red Hen appeared in 2010. He is currently at work on paintings, collages and unique books, continuing his life-long exploration of visual poetry.

Photograph by George Evans at the Whisky A Go Go, 1986.

Over breakfast in Eugene, Oregon, 2006.
Photograph by Penelope Patrick Oshatz

More Praise for Wanda Coleman & Austin Straus

"If our world revolved around Straus and Coleman, there would be no need for Venus, other planets or stars. This is a book of feelings and not just words. Tenderness can be found throughout *The Love Project*. This is not hit-and-run loving. This is Watts undressing for Brooklyn. It's a husband and wife leaving teeth marks and a place for tongues on this institution we call marriage. What is poetry without intimacy? Straus and Coleman is that couple holding hands after the movies. Desire is the place they call home."
—**E. Ethelbert Miller, author of *How We Sleep on the Nights We Don't Make Love***

"This collection is an impassioned love duet on steroids, a feast of contemporary love poems by two highly engaging and accomplished poets who are lifetime soul-mates. Wanda Coleman's complex black L.A. muse sings 'a rich mutual insatiable lust,' so transporting that 'even jazz can't go there,' while Austin Straus's dead-ahead Brooklyn Jewish muse laughs out loud with delineating 'how our bodies glow together,' and announces with exuberant delight: 'I love the way you ruin my day!'"
—**Steve Kowit, author of *The Dumbbell Nebula* and *The First Noble Truth***

"The paradox of Wanda Coleman is that despite her underclass stance and winks from the bottom of the racial and economic deck, she is perhaps L.A.'s most nationally prominent poet. . . . The quality of her work transcends the socio-politics of modern literary multicultural America. . . . She is the real thing . . . a sophisticated beat hipster with echoes of Ginsberg, Blake, and Hughes."
—***Vice & Verse***

"Austin Straus has been a missionary for the poetry movement since he first started writing in 1976. He read a poem to an audience and was surprised to learn 'they liked what I wrote.' In addition to being entertaining, Straus feels poetry encourages creativity."
—***The Larchmont Chronicle***

"Few contemporary poets can match the honesty and anguished yet celebratory fierceness of Coleman's vernacular and highly literary voice."
—**Judges' Statement, The Shelley Memorial Award, Poetry Society of America, 2012**

"Translating their marriage into poetry, Wanda Coleman and Austin Straus have composed an unsettling love potion of inner demons, tumultuous 'scènes de ménage,' euphoric portraits of each other, and succulent make-up sex. These writings are not for the faint of heart.

—**Alta Ifland, author of** *Death-in-a-Box* **and** *The Snail's Song*

"Looking at his striking mixed media collages, you can see that it's appropriate for the spoken word to be part of the program because questions, names, letters, words, and phrases are important elements in these works [by Austin Straus] . . . that embrace both the poet and the painter within. . . ."

—*Eugene Weekly,* **April 2001**

"The marriage of true minds, it turns out, does admit impediment—as well as dispute, desolation, distance—when, as Straus puts it, 'the hot dump we call home fills with blood.' *The Love Project* admits all—mutual admiration, intimate babble they dub 'Deep English,' pet names for sundry nooks of each others' bodies, laughter that binds, an ongoing magnetism of desire pulling them back together again and again. And, above all, the consolation of abiding love, 'love at the door pounding, eager to help him remember forever who he is, who they can be together.' Between them, Coleman and Straus ravel a gorgeous document, a full-color rendering of their long relationship—not a stable portrait, but a volatile, ever-changing one that returns always to the gift each tenders the other. Coleman says it perhaps most succinctly, 'not gravity. love/weights me to earth.' The authors of these offerings have taken the enormous risk of opening their most intimate selves to us. Pure and simple, this book brings hope."

—**Marsha de la O, author of** *Black Hope,* **and Phil Taggart, author of** *Opium Wars,* **wife and husband, coeditors of** *Askew*

"No easy remedy for the lacerating American concerns of racism and gender bias, Coleman's poetry transforms pain into empathy. . . . These searing, soaring poems challenge us to repair the fractures of human difference, and feel what it is to be made whole again."

—**Judges' Statement for** *Mercurochrome,* **The National Book Award, 2001**

Wanda Coleman and Austin Straus
would have celebrated thirty-three years together on
May 1st, 2014.